W9-CUI-064

Lerner SPORTS

BEHIND THE SCENES
BASEBALL

by James Monson

Lerner Publications ◆ Minneapolis

Lerner Publications Company
A division of Lerner Publishing Group, Inc.
241 First Avenue North
Minneapolis, MN 55401 USA

For reading levels and more information, look up this title at www.lernerbooks.com.

The images in this book are used with the permission of: © Rob Tringali/MLB Photos/Getty Images, p. 1; © Ezra Shaw/Getty Images Sport/Getty Images, pp. 4–5, p. 6; © tammykayphoto/Shutterstock.com, pp. 8–9, 29; © Scott W. Grau/Icon Sportswire/Getty Images, pp. 10–11; © Stephen Lew/Icon Sportswire/Corbis/Getty Images, p. 12; © Zachary Roy/Getty Images Sport/Getty Images, p. 13; © Billie Weiss/Boston Red Sox/Getty Images Sport/Getty Images, pp. 14–15; © Rob Tringali/MLB Photos/Getty Images, p. 16; © Sarah Sachs/Arizona Diamondbacks/Getty Images Sport/Getty Images, p. 18; © Michael Zagaris/Oakland Athletics/Getty Images Sport/Getty Images, pp. 20–21; © Keeton Gale/Shutterstock.com, pp. 22–23; © Mark Cunningham/MLB Photos/Getty Images Sport/Getty Images, pp. 24–25; © Gabe Souza/Portland Press Herald/Getty Images, p. 26.

Front Cover: © Rob Tringali/MLB Photos/Getty Images.

Main body text set in Myriad Pro.
Typeface provided by Adobe.

Library of Congress Cataloging-in-Publication Data

Names: Monson, James, 1994– author.
Title: Behind the scenes baseball / James Monson.
Description: Minneapolis : Lerner Publications, [2020] | Series: Inside the sport | Includes bibliographical references and index. | Audience: Age 7–11. | Audience: Grade 4 to 6.
Identifiers: LCCN 2018050533 (print) | LCCN 2018055121 (ebook) | ISBN 9781541556263 (eb pdf) | ISBN 9781541556065 (lib) | ISBN 9781541574342 (pbk)
Subjects: LCSH: Baseball—Training—Juvenile literature. | Baseball players—Health and hygiene—Juvenile literature. | Baseball players—United States—Conduct of life—Juvenile literature. | Baseball players—United States—Charitable contributions—Juvenile literature. | Major League Baseball—Juvenile literature.
Classification: LCC GV867.5 (ebook) | LCC GV867.5 .M64 2020 (print) | DDC 796.357—dc23

LC record available at https://lccn.loc.gov/2018050533

Manufactured in the United States of America
2-48602-43478-10/10/2019

CONTENTS

GETTING TO THE TOP

George Springer of the Houston Astros stepped up to the plate. He had waited his entire life for this moment. It was Game 7 of the 2017 World Series of Major League Baseball (MLB).

The Astros were already ahead of the Los Angeles Dodgers 3–0 in the second inning. Still, Springer could help his team with a hit. There was a runner on third base. Dodgers pitcher Yu Darvish needed one more strike to get Springer out.

Darvish threw the ball. The pitch was low, but Springer was ready. He put all his might into the swing.

George Springer scores a run, helping the Houston Astros win the 2017 World Series. ▶

FACTS
at a Glance

- Players as young as eighteen years old can be drafted by MLB teams.

- The Little League World Series is one of the top tournaments for young baseball players. It takes place each year in Williamsport, Pennsylvania.

- Most baseball players get to the stadium four or more hours before a game to get ready.

- The MLB season starts for most players in February when they go to spring training. Teams either practice in Arizona or Florida because of the warm weather.

- The MLB regular season is long. Teams usually play at least six games per week.

Springer celebrates with his teammate ▶ Carlos Correa.

His swing sent the ball soaring into the air. The Los Angeles outfielders ran back to the fence, but the ball was gone. Home run! Springer rounded the bases, pumping his fists and cheering. The Dodgers' fans were shocked. It was now 5–0 Houston. The entire Astros team cheered as Springer crossed home plate.

In the ninth inning, it was official. The Astros got their final out and won the World Series. Springer had a big smile on his face as he hugged his teammates to celebrate.

Springer and many other MLB players work hard from a young age to make it to the pros. Once they get there, the goal is to win the World Series. Players must put in work almost every day in order to accomplish their goals like Springer did.

CHAPTER 1

RISING UP THE RANKS

The path to the pros for many baseball players starts at a young age. Many play tee ball when they are four or five years old. Then coaches begin to pitch to the young hitters. Eventually, the players begin to pitch.

The top players usually start playing on traveling teams when they are about ten years old. These teams are based out of certain cities but can end up going long distances for tournaments. The top youth tournament happens each year in Williamsport, Pennsylvania. It's called the Little League World Series and features some of the world's best twelve- and thirteen-year-old baseball players.

Young baseball players can practice throwing, hitting, catching, and baserunning. ▶

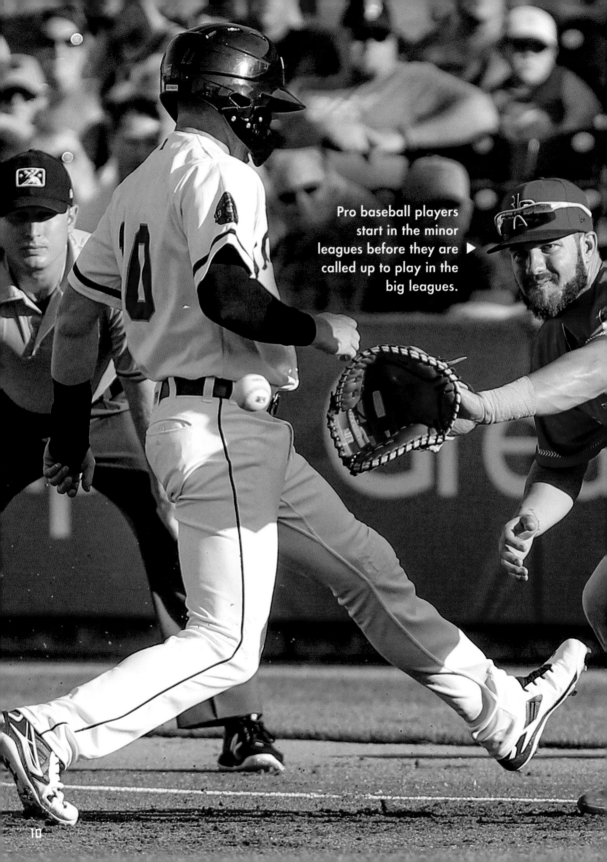

Pro baseball players start in the minor leagues before they are ▶ called up to play in the big leagues.

Players are scouted in their early high school years. MLB and college scouts travel the country looking for up-and-coming stars. The MLB Draft happens each June. Teams have their pick of eighteen-year-old and college-age players. Many of the top players will be drafted when they are eighteen years old. Once drafted, a player usually has the option to either join the team's minor league system or go to college. If a player goes to college, he can reenter the draft after his junior year and be selected by a new team.

The path from the minors to the majors can be a long one. Many players never make it to the major leagues. Each MLB team has at least five minor league teams. Most players start at rookie ball. They work their way up from low Class A to high Class A to Class AA to Class AAA.

The Iowa Cubs are a minor league team just one step below the major leagues. They're connected to the Chicago Cubs.

If a player is good enough, he will end up being called up to the major league team. Many players need about five years to get all the way through the minors and onto the major league roster, but some make it to the major leagues faster than that. Bryce Harper joined the Washington Nationals after spending two seasons in the minor leagues.

The Portland Sea Dogs are a minor league team connected to the Boston Red Sox.

CHAPTER 2

FROM BED TO THE BATTER'S BOX

Most MLB games are played at night, starting around 7:00 p.m. local time. But the day for a professional baseball player begins in the morning. Most players wake up somewhere between 8:00 and 10:00 a.m. for a night game. No matter what time it is, players try to sleep the same number of hours each night.

For night games, players usually have some time to prepare at home or at their hotel before heading to the ballpark. They eat a light, healthful breakfast, such as an omelet with veggies or lean meat. Most players arrive at the stadium around 1:00 or 2:00 p.m.

Drew Pomeranz of the Boston Red Sox walks into the dugout before a game. ▶

Yasiel Puig of the Los Angeles Dodgers takes batting practice before a game.

There, the first thing that happens is lunch. Some players pick up food at a restaurant on the way. Others will eat at the ballpark. Many players eat salads or sandwiches.

Players then change into workout clothes and running shoes. They head out onto the field and stretch. Next, they work on fielding with a coach or practice hitting in the batting cage.

In the hour or two before the game, players head to the clubhouse to have their pregame meal. The food there includes fruits and vegetables, along with toppings for sandwiches. Some players then play cards or video games to relax and take their minds off of the upcoming game. Others will watch videos of themselves or their opponents playing to prepare. Players at an away game might call friends or family on the phone.

When it's game time, the players are ready. Throughout the game, each player is focused on helping his team win.

Stats Spotlight
90 to 120

That's the average number of baseballs used in an MLB game. Balls are usually taken out of the game when they become too dirty for the pitchers and hitters. Home runs and foul balls also fly into the stands. Players like to toss the ball to a fan after catching the last out of an inning. A single ball lasts an average of three pitches before it is taken out of the game.

Taijuan Walker of the Arizona Diamondbacks is interviewed at his locker after a game. ▼

Still, the players try to have fun while working hard. They do this by having secret handshakes or making jokes with their teammates. Didi Gregorius of the New York Yankees does a different handshake with each one of his teammates.

When the final out is made, it's back into the clubhouse. Media reporters interview the players at their lockers. During the playoffs, players usually go to another room and sit at a table with microphones to answer questions from many reporters at once.

Once they're done with interviews, some players will work out. Others will go straight for the postgame buffet. The buffet food may change depending on the team, but is usually a meal from a restaurant. It can be barbecue, sushi, or another kind of meal.

Then it's time for players to head home or to the hotel after a long day at the ballpark. Soon it will be time for another game, and they will do the same routine all over again.

CHAPTER 3

NO TIME TO WASTE

The MLB season starts in late March and can go until the beginning of November. There are games almost every day. Players usually have one day off per week. They have to use their time off wisely to stay healthy and fit.

Players often work out in their free time. They want to stay as fit as possible. Another thing baseball players do in their free time is watch videos of games. They want to see how they can play better.

Baseball players make sure they get enough sleep each night. They need energy to be ready on game day.

Henderson Alvarez of the Oakland Athletics studies videos to learn how he can improve his game. ▶

During spring training,
◀ MLB teams play games
to sharpen their skills.

They also spend time recovering after games. Some do this by getting massages or acupuncture.

In January players start getting ready for the season. They do light workouts and try to improve their throwing or hitting skills. Spring training for most teams starts in February. Teams practice in either Arizona or Florida. They go to these southern states because of the warm winter weather.

Players use spring training as a way to prepare for the season. New technology has helped. Teams can now put sensors on bats so they can see how the ball hits off a player's bat. Other sensors can track the rotation of a pitch, how much energy a player is using, and more.

New technology can also help protect players. Many players wear extra gear to protect themselves if they are hit by a pitch. Some batters wear a larger helmet flap to protect their face if a ball hits them there. Some pitchers also wear helmets.

CHAPTER 4

AWAY FROM THE FIELD

The MLB regular season usually ends around October 1. Teams that make it to the playoffs might play until early November. Once the season is over, it's time to relax. Many players want to spend time with their families. They spend a lot of time away from family during the season because they travel to games.

The winter is a quiet time for many baseball players. Some players do charity work. Most teams have a fan festival that players attend to meet with fans. It's a good way for fans to get to know the players.

James McCann of the Detroit Tigers takes a selfie with fans. ▶

A Trenton Thunder minor league player waits for a pitch with 12 seconds on the pitch clock.

This helps fans get excited about the upcoming season. Players usually sign autographs and take photos with fans.

MLB is always working to promote its players and games. Teams use social media to show what players are like off the field. MLB has also used technology to give fans more ways to watch the games. Many fans can now watch their favorite team on their cell phone or tablet. MLB has shown some of its games on Facebook.

On the field, MLB is working to make the game more interesting for fans. In 2015, minor league teams started using pitch clocks, which give pitchers a time limit for throwing their pitches. The goal is to speed up the game and make sure fans aren't waiting long to see the action. MLB teams hope to continue finding new ways to bring more fans to baseball.

Stats Spotlight
$2.2 Million

That's the amount of money Anthony Rizzo of the Chicago Cubs raised through his charity foundation in 2017. The foundation raised money for children fighting cancer. Rizzo himself is a cancer survivor. He was diagnosed in 2008, when he was a young minor league baseball player.

YOUR TURN

Some of the best baseball players are also some of the best base runners. Being able to run the bases well can help players score extra runs for their teams. One way young players can practice this skill is by doing relay baserunning.

Get together with a group of friends. First, divide the group into two teams. One team will head to second base while the other team goes to home plate. Each team should line up in a single-file line. The player at the front of each line should have a baseball in his hand. Someone starts the drill by saying, "Go!" The player on each team with the ball starts running around the bases. They run all the way around to their original base.

When the player gets back to their original base, he hands off the baseball to the next person in line. She does the exact same thing. The first team to have all of its players run around

Young baseball players want to make sure they can run fast enough to score.

the bases wins. This drill is the perfect chance for friends to have

fun racing while also becoming faster base runners.

GLOSSARY

acupuncture
a way to relieve pain by pushing needles into certain parts of a person's skin

batting cage
an area surrounded by a fence or net where players can practice hitting

buffet
a meal that people can serve themselves, usually with a large selection of foods

charity
related to an organization that gives money or services to those in need

clubhouse
a place where baseball players spend time before and after games

fielding
playing infield and outfield positions in baseball

playoffs
the end of the season when the top teams compete for the championship

rotation
the act of something moving around a central point

routine
a set of actions done in the same order

scouted
watched by a scout, who judges someone's skills and ability to play a certain sport

sensors
devices that can track stats instantly

tee ball
a variation of baseball in which players hit the ball off a tee instead of being pitched to

FURTHER
INFORMATION

Baseball America
http://www.baseballamerica.com

Fishman, Jon. *Baseball's G.O.A.T.: Babe Ruth, Mike Trout, and More*. Minneapolis:
    Lerner Publications, 2020.

Major League Baseball
https://www.mlb.com

Morey, Allan. *Baseball Records*. Minneapolis: Bellwether Media, Inc., 2018.

National Baseball Hall of Fame
https://baseballhall.org

Savage, Jeff. *Baseball Super Stats*. Minneapolis: Lerner Publications, 2018.

INDEX

ABOUT THE AUTHOR

James Monson is a sportswriter based in the Minneapolis-Saint Paul area. He has written articles that have appeared in various publications across the country. He has a degree in print/digital sports journalism.